# The First Lady of
# W A I K I K I
## A PICTORIAL HISTORY OF THE
# *Sheraton*
# *Moana Surfrider*

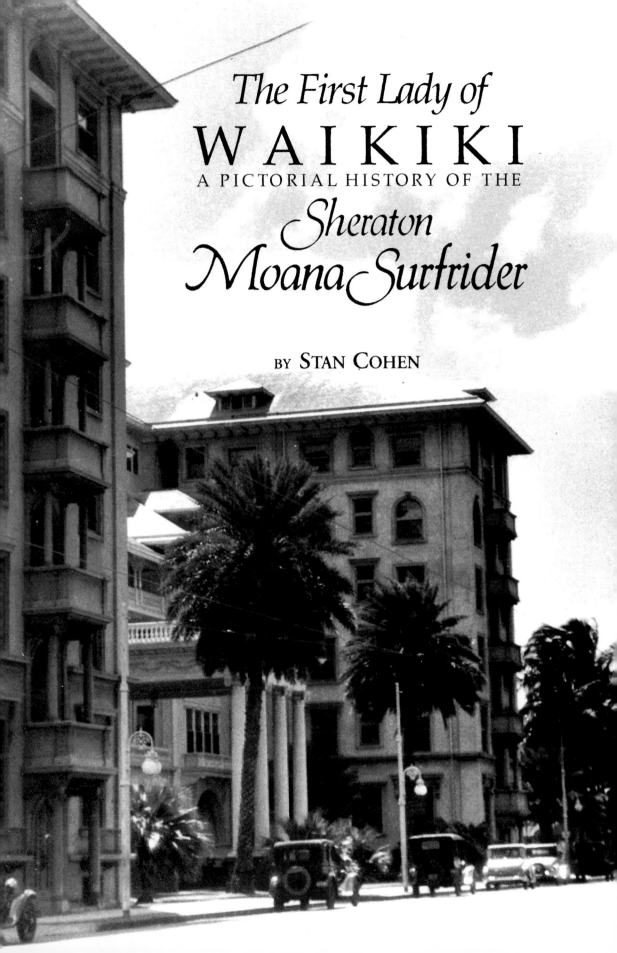

# The First Lady of
# WAIKIKI
## A PICTORIAL HISTORY OF THE
## *Sheraton*
## *Moana Surfrider*

BY STAN COHEN

LIBRARY OF CONGRESS
CATALOG CARD NO. 95-71786

ISBN 1-57510-008-8

PRINTED IN U.S.A.

First Printing: December 1995
Second Printing: February 2000

*Typography:* Leslie R. Maricelli
*Cover Art Work:* Mike Egeler, Egeler Design

PICTORIAL HISTORIES PUBLISHING COMPANY, INC.
*713 South Third St. West,*
*Missoula Montana 59801*

# Introduction

Thousands of people pass by the Sheraton Moana Surfrider on Kalakaua Avenue every year without realizing the historic significance of the property. This book will hopefully correct this. The main 1901 building and 1918 wing additions have been overshadowed by the high rises surrounding them, but the architectural features of the structure have not been lost. Special recognition is extended to the owners of the hotel, Kyo-ya, Co., Ltd., for their foresight in restoring *The First Lady of Waikiki*. Their sensitivity to the issue of preservation has saved an important piece of Hawaii's history so that generations can enjoy her charm and elegance for years to come. The hotel now takes its place among America's leading hotels listed in the National Register of Historic Places.

Hawaii's former Governor John Waihee and his wife, Lynn accept the Moana key from hotel owner Masakuni Osano (left) and Mrs. Eiko Osano, widow of Kenji Osano. Over a period of 30 years Kenji Osano amassed a financial conglomerate in three countries which included transportation, real estate, auto franchises and hotels. In 1963 Osano bought the three Sheraton Hotels in Waikiki: the Moana and Surfrider Hotels and the Sheraton Princess Kaiulani. MH

# CONTENTS

# ACKNOWLEDGMENTS

This book could not have been produced without the help and encouragement of Barbara Sheehan, former Director of Public Relations, Sheraton Moana Surfrider Resort and her staff. A vast amount of photos and written information was obtained from the hotel's historical files. I also would like to thank the staffs of the Bishop Museum and Hawaii Archives for help with photos. And a special thank you to DeSoto Brown of Honolulu who again gave me access to his extensive collection of Hawaiian memorabilia. Thanks also to Don Medcalf of Honolulu for the use of the Moana Hotel Company's stock certificate and to David Franzen and Christopher Irion for use of the new color photos.

# PHOTO SOURCES

BM — Bishop Museum Archives, Honolulu
MH — Sheraton Moana Surfrider Archives
HA — Hawaii State Archives, Honolulu
DB — DeSoto Brown Collection, Honolulu
Other photos credited to their source.

# THE FIRST LADY OF WAIKIKI

In the late 1890s Waikiki was a quiet backwater area, surrounded by swamps, taro fields and mosquito-infested duck ponds, but with a beautiful beach, three miles from the center of Honolulu. It was connected to the city by the Waikiki Road, which had a horse-drawn train terminating at Kapiolani Park.

Waikiki was the site of homes of Hawaiian royalty and wealthy kamaainas including the magnificent home of W.C. Peacock. A 300-foot pier had been built about 1890 out into the ocean near the Peacock residence. At its end was a covered pavilion.

Visitors to the island at this time had to stay in Honolulu and venture out to the beaches of Waikiki daily as there were no real accommodations in the beach area. Investors were reluctant to invest their money in Waikiki because of the distance from Honolulu and the aforementioned topographical features.

There were, however, several small tourist sites available in the Waikiki area catering mostly to the local trade. One of the most notable was the Sans Souci built in 1884 by Allen Herbert, who named it after Frederick the Great's palace. The hotel was actually a series of small bungalows and Robert Louis Stevenson spent time there on several of his island trips. (It is speculative whether he actually spent time writing under the Moana's famous banyan tree, as has been reported).

By the late 1890s, with additional steamship lines calling at Honolulu, "the inflow of tourists was rapidly becoming greater and greater. It was not unusual to see businessmen from the mainland who had come here principally for the waters of Waikiki," stated the *Hawaiian Almanac*.

In 1896, Walter C. Peacock proposed to build Waikiki's first real hotel to provide a solution to the area's main drawback—the lack of suitable accommodations on the beach.

His corporation, The Moana Hotel Company, Ltd., commissioned architect Oliver G. Traphagen to draw up a plan to renovate the Peacock home and build guest cottages on the grounds. Traphagen, from Duluth, Minnesota, became enchanted with Hawaii and designed a number of the island's buildings and homes.

After a number of delays and changes, the Peacock home was moved to another location and construction began in September 1899 on a four-story, 75-room building. The Lucas Brothers, who also built the Iolani Palace, were the prime contractors.

The architect used selected aspects of the Beaux-Arts style developed in Europe in the last half of the 19th century.

The Moana Hotel Company, Ltd., began with capital of $100,000 (money given to Walter Peacock by his sister, Annie) which was later increased to $150,000. Opening on March 11, 1901, the Moana, which means "broad expanse of ocean," was one of Oahu's tallest and most elaborate buildings. Ionic columns supported an elegant porte cochere at the entrance leading to a lobby resplendent in detailed millwork. The coffered lobby ceiling was embellished with intricate plaster detailing. Each guest floor was furnished in a different fine wood—oak, mahogany or maple. Each guest room had a telephone and private bath, true innovations at the time. The first floor had a billiard room, saloon, parlor, library, office and reception area, plus the Territory's first electric-powered elevator. A rooftop observatory 120 feet above offered dancing and 360-degree views of Diamond Head, the plains and the ocean. The dining room extended over the water and the hotel had its own ice plant and electric generators.

The hotel site just before construction commenced in 1899. The large house known as the Peacock House was moved to make way for the new hotel. The beachhouse, to the left, remained in place and was used for some years as a beach facility for hotel guests. MH

# W.C. Peacock

*Walter Chamberlain Peacock, the visionary behind the original Moana Hotel was born in England in 1858, one of four children. Walter settled first in Australia and then California. His brothers, Frank and Corbet joined him, impressed with Walter's stories of the great wealth and opportunity in America. Frank was later killed in Wyoming, and Walter and Corbet ventured forth to Hawaii, settling on Oahu to pursue their fortunes.*

*The two brothers founded W.C. Peacock and Company, Ltd., and proceeded to obtain licenses to run liquor establishments (saloons) all over downtown Honolulu. The business was extremely successful but Walter saw other opportunities for investment in the islands.*

*In 1896, he formed The Moana Hotel Company to develop a major resort hotel at a Waikiki Beach location. The hotel was an immediate success after its opening in 1901.*

*Walter had many interests and passions, and he and Corbet were also successful in the farming equipment industry. They traveled to Australia and introduced the first steel plow, "The Peacock Plow" to that country.*

*Walter eventually sold his interest in the hotel and he died in 1909 at age 50.*

W.C. Peacock MH

The hotel's first guests in 1901 were a group of 114 Shriners hosted by the local Aloha Temple Shriners. The guests were presented with fezzes made of native Lauhala or brown fiber from which hung a tassel of coconut fiber. They paid a pricey $1.50 per night for their rooms.

After the hotel opened, the owners saw the main selling point was the hotel's location on the beach. Another plus was its location on the tram line leading to downtown Honolulu, three miles away. In 1905, Peacock sold the hotel to Alexander Young, a prominent Honolulu businessman with other island hotel interests. After Young's death in 1910, his estate continued to operate the hotel until the Matson Navigation Company bought it in 1932.

The Moana became the center of Waikiki's growing popularity in the early 1900s. By 1918, Hawaii had 8,000 visitors annually and, responding to this growth in visitors, a massive addition was built. Two floors were added along with concrete wings on each side designed in the Italian Renaissance style. This more than doubled the size of the hotel and created the distinctive "H" shape it has today. All components were integrated with a series of recurring archways in halls, windows and entries. The large Banyan tree behind the hotel separated the two wings and became the famous Banyan Court with lanais on its three sides. It has been a favorite outdoor dining spot for generations of Honolulu's citizens and visitors.

In the 1920s Matson Navigation Company ships were bringing growing numbers of wealthy visitors. The building of the Ala Wai Canal brought an end to the swamps and mosquitoes in the area. The opening of The Royal Hawaiian Hotel in 1927, just a few blocks from the Moana, helped alleviate the shortage of rooms in Waikiki.

Both hotels attracted the well-traveled and well-heeled. In 1920, the young Prince of Wales (who became King of England and later the Duke of Windsor) stayed at the Moana with his cousin Lord Louis Mountbatten as part of an around-the-world tour. They spent much of their time dancing at the hotel and were particularly taken with the latest song "Hula Blues," written by the hotel's orchestra leader, Johnny Noble.

The 1920s were a romantic era for the Moana and Hawaii. Writer, Art Wyeth in his "As I Remember" column recalled those nostalgic days and nights at the hotel:

*"We used to gather there for dancing on the lanai and dinner, if our wallets were full enough. There was a long pier which jutted out into the ocean with a square pavilion at the end. Here the tourists and townspeople gathered to hear the beachboys strumming on their ukuleles and guitars under a full moon. I can still go back to those very vivid memories, of those perfect nights with the moon shining down on an almost flat sea with the splash of a tiny wave feeling its way onto the beach. Lovers strolled under the spell of moonlight that only Hawaii can produce."*

Other notable visitors and celebrities through the years included Amelia Earhart, Walter Chrysler, Joe DiMaggio, Frank Sinatra, Boris Karloff, Loretta Young, Broderick Crawford and Lucille Ball, among others.

In 1932, the Matson Steamship Company, Hawaii's predominant passenger carrier, purchased the Moana Hotel for $1.6 million. They had constructed the premier hotel in Hawaii at the time, The Royal Hawaiian, in 1927. Both hotels, plus the Seaside Bungalows and the Waialae Ranch Company were under the umbrella of the Territorial Hotel Company, Ltd. The Moana received a complete renovation in 1928, 10 years after the two concrete wings were added.

The Territorial Hotel Company was liquidated in 1933 and the hotels were turned over to Hawaiian Properties with some of the same partners. This company was in turn liquidated in 1941 and the hotels division of Matson assumed full control of all properties.

From 1941 to January 1945, Arthur Benaglia, who was the general manager of the Royal for 17 years, was also manager of the Moana.

Tourism boomed in Hawaii in the late 1940s and 1950s with the advent of regularly scheduled airline services from the west coast. Matson continued to service its hotels with passenger service until it sold all its hotel properties on Waikiki to the Sheraton Hotel chain in 1959. This was also the year Hawaii became the 50th state and the first year of jet airline service to the islands.

Sheraton in turn sold the Moana and The Royal Hawaiian to Japanese industrialist, Kenji Osano and his Kyo-Ya Company, Ltd., in 1974, but continues to manage them under a long-term contract.

In keeping with modern trends, there were several renovations over the years to reflect up-to-date architectural images and innovations. This included the removal of the porte cochere and installation of an entry awning. Original exterior Colonial banisters, detailed millwork and verandas were also removed. In the 1930s high ceilings were dropped and changes to the interior design were made reflecting less of the original Colonial period design and more of a modern Art Deco style. Further updating occurred in the late 1950s and early 1960s.

In 1977, Sheraton began a major renovation costing $1 million to bring back the graceful decor of the early years. Flooring and carpeting reminiscent of the original design were installed in the lobby and hallways. The rooms were renovated and many were furnished with period Victorian furniture. Some of the ornate original woodwork was uncovered and the airy design was brought back.

But the hotel would not be completely returned to its early 1900s elegance until the extensive, $50 million renovation which was completed in 1989.

The architect's rendering of the first tourist-oriented hotel to be built in Waikiki.
NA C.B. Wood Coll. #21,732

Opening day for the elegant Moana Hotel, March 11, 1901. The hotel will celebrate its 100-year anniversary of hosting visitors from all over the world in 2001. MH

Four sailors on the pier fronting the Moana Hotel, circa 1920. BM CP73439

## THE MOANA PIER

*One of the most popular attractions on Waikiki Beach in the early days was a pier built around 1890 on property owned by Walter Peacock. The pier jutted out into the water 300 feet and has a small pavilion on the end. It became known as the Moana Pier after the hotel opened in 1901.*

*On the sides of the pavilion were two boat davits used to hold small boats sent out from foreign warships anchored off Waikiki.*

*From the Banyan Court guests would stroll out on the pier to listen to the impromptu singing of Hawaiian music groups and amateurs playing ukuleles and guitars. Romantic couples would stroll out to watch the moonlight on the water.*

*Tourists thronged to see the musicians and singers including the Kahanamoku brothers, David, Sam and Bill, younger brothers of Duke Kahanamoku, Olympic swimming great and surfing champion.*

*By 1930, the pier was declared unsafe by the Board of Harbor Commissioners and was demolished. The Paradise of the Pacific magazine wrote: "Another link between the romantic past of Honolulu and the more or less romantic present of this mid-Pacific city has passed away. The old Moana Pier, on which a thousand romances have begun and perhaps as many dissolved, has been torn down."*

January 22, 1897.

W. C. PEACOCK ESQ.,

Honolulu.

Sir:-

Referring to the matter of application for a Spirit
License for the proposed new Hotel at Waikiki, I am now
directed by the Minister of the Interior to say that at a
meeting of the Executive Council held January 20th inst,
it was resolved to allow Mr. Peacock a license to furnish
"liquor, according to the former statement, to the regular
"guests of the hotel and to those registering and taking
"regular meals, the meaning of regular meal being a meal
"that is regularly served in the course of the conduct of
"the Hotel; also it is required that the establishment shall
"have not less than thirty (30) well appointed and furnished
"sleeping rooms for guests.   The form of the bond and the
"license to be submitted to the Executive Council to be
"approved of."

"The condition to be embodied:  that upon a breach
"of any of the conditions the license shall be forfeited
"by the licensee."

A copy of the former statement herein referred to is
enclosed herewith.

I have the honor to be
Your Obedient Servant,
J. A. Hassinger
Chief Clerk.

No.

*Incorporated under the Laws of the Hawaiian Islands*

— Shares —

# The Moana Hotel Company, Limited

Capital Stock $100,000

1,000 Shares, $100 each

This is to Certify that

Honolulu, H. I.

is the owner of

Shares of

The Moana Hotel Company, Limited

*Transferable on the books of the Company by endorsement hereon and surrender of this Certificate.*

Treasurer.

President.

Stock issued by The Moana Hotel
Company, Ltd., in 1900.

Don Medcalf Coll., Honolulu

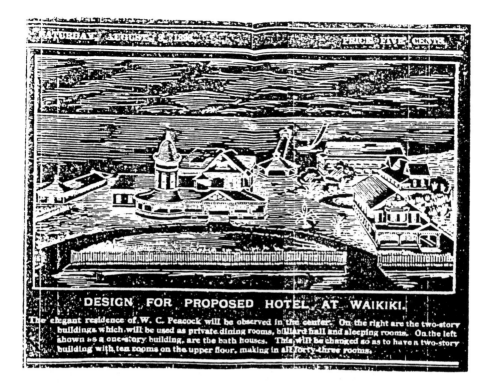

This drawing appeared in a Honolulu newspaper on Aug. 8, 1896. The caption stated: The elegant residence of W.C. Peacock will be observed in the center. On the right are the two-story buildings which will be used as private dining rooms, billiard hall and sleeping rooms. On the left shown as a one-story building, are the bath houses. This will be changed as to have a two-story building with ten rooms on the upper floor, making in all forty-three rooms.

One of the attractions for placing the hotel at this location was the street car line which ran on Kalakaua Avenue (formerly Waikiki Road), connecting Waikiki with downtown Honolulu, circa 1905. The line was mule-drawn until electrified in 1903. MH

# MOANA HOTEL OPENED LAST EVENING
# WITH GLITTER AND GOOD CHEER

THE LOBBY

THE DINING ROOM.

## SCENES IN THE NEW MOANA HOTEL.

AMID the sounding swash of the surf on the sands of Waikiki, the strains of music and to the clinking of glasses of bubbling wine, the beautiful Moana hotel at Waikiki was christened last night. Moana, known far and wide among the Polynesians and to every race in the Pacific ocean as the "broad expanse of the ocean," was a fit cognomen for the magnificent hostelry which was dedicated as a resting place for the tourists of the wide, wide world who visit the Paradise of the Pacific.

Illuminated by the glow of thousands of electric, parti-hued globes, magnificent of exterior and interior and bearing in every detail the stately outlines of the old Colonial period, the now hostelry rivalled even the finest hotels which are to be seen in the most metropolitan cities on the mainland or on the continent. From the highest pinnacle of the observatory lanai, lighted by scores of red, white and blue globes, to the basement where were stored amid Arctic frosts edibles to pamper the most epicurean of tastes, there was nothing to criticise except that it be up praise.

Never was a house of good cheer christened amid more auspicious circumstances. The banquet which was complimentary to the press of Honolulu was attended by Honolulu's representative business men and the clinking of champagne glasses betokened the fact that Honolulu had at last become metropolitan indeed.

Furnished throughout with rare taste, in which the Colonial style predominates, the rooms of each floor of the hotel are models of neatness and convenience. Every comfort which can be found in the hotels of the mainland is to be found at the Moana. Be it in the spacious halls, carpeted with the softest of plush or velvet carpets, in the large, airy rooms, in which only the choicest of Colonial designs of chairs, chiffonieres, writing desks and tables are to be found, or the dining room with its expanse of floor, open to every breeze which may float in from the ocean or from the valleys, the hotel is complete in every detail.

Promptly at 6:30 o'clock the automobiles, gratuitously supplied by Manager Grant of the Hawaiian Automobile Company, carried the guests of Mr. J. G. Rothwell, director of the Moana Hotel Company, to the beach. The guests were shown through the various floors and hotel departments by "Bob" Scott, the chief clerk, who is well known

to the traveling public. The guests were greeted to a surprise upon alighting from the cabs under the Colonial porte cochere and upon entering the rotunda, where clerk's office, elevator and cloak rooms are located. This, together with the hallways, billiard rooms, buffet and ladies' parlor, are finished in oak, the modified Colonial style predominating. Among the most attractive features are the Doric and Ionic pillars and the pilasters, crowned with carved oak capitals. From the rotunda is a wide hallway leading to the reading and writing room and the ladies' parlor. The latter is a beautiful retiring place, supplied with exquisite furniture of the Martha Washington period. The tables, chairs and settees are inlaid with mother-of-pearl in scroll designs. Soft plush carpets cover the polished floor.

The second level of the hotel is called the "Oak Floor." Every piece of furniture is of oak, in quaint designs. Each bedroom is supplied with brass bedsteads, many sorts being distributed on the various floors. Marble stationary washstands are found in every room. One of the conveniences is that each room opens into the next, although all can be closed against each other by a series of patent locks.

The third floor is termed the "Mahogany Floor," each room being furnished with settings of that wood.

The fourth floor is the "Maple Floor." Surmounting the whole, and reached by the elevator, is the observatory lanai, studded with electric lights in the hues of the national colors.

O. G. Traphagen, the architect of the building, spent much time in studying the features of Colonial architecture best adapted to the climate of the Hawaiian Islands. The building was designed for Honolulu alone. It was dif-

ficult to adhere to any strict method of architecture for such a climate and there is no hotel on the face of the globe which is similar in outline. Mr. Traphagen does not believe that any of a purely Colonial style compares with it. The interior wood finish is of oak, with Georgia pine and Nor'-west pine finishings. The first story is finished throughout in white oak.

Catton, Neill & Co. installed the power, ice plant and electric generators, the Oceanic Gas and Electric Company putting in the electric connections, room telephones and fixtures. One room can be connected with another by means of the telephone system. The hotel has its own power house and laundry of the latest conveniences and cold storage plant.

The guests last evening were escorted to the dining room, which is erected almost over the waters which roll in unceasingly with a boom which will be music to the ears of the diners. The tables for the banquet, which was complimentary to the Honolulu press, were arranged in the form of a hollow square and were covered by chaste designs of Colonial silverware and the whitest of napery. The coolest of breezes floated in from mountain and sea.

Mr. J. G. Rothwell occupied the head of the tables and flanking him were the following guests: J. A. McCandless, Andrew Brown, Theodore Lansing, Commodore Beckley, A. E. Kaeser, W. R. Farrington, F. J. Cross, Robert Catton, John Neill, Lewis Gear, O. G. Traphagen, J. F. Humburg, Frank Hustace, J. Bicknell, L. V. Grant, Edward Dekum, R. O. Yardley, J. D. McInerny, Captain Schaefer, F. E. Richardson, A. V. Gear, C. H. Morton, James Bergstrom, Frank Hoogs, Charles Weight, "Bob" Scott, Charles Lu-

cas, Tom Lucas, C. L. Rhodes of Star, W. H. Coney of the Bulletin, Edmund Norrie of the Independent, A. Taylor of the Advertiser, R. Beverley Kidd, Star.

Addresses were made by Theodore Lansing, J. G. Rothwell, C. L. Rhodes, Frank Hoogs, Andrew Brown, Tom Lucas, Commodore Beckley, A. E. Kaeser, R. Beverley Kidd, L. T. Grant, A. V. Gear, Clinton Hutchins and others.

Mr. Rothwell has chosen for his manager F. M. Smith, manager, who has been connected with the Occidental hotel, San Francisco; "Bob" Scott, formerly of the Hawaiian, chief clerk; W. Zabriskie, night clerk; Miss Ju Cook, bookkeeper and cashier; Marcel Magnan, chef; St. Clair Bidgood, dining room steward. The banquet was overflowing with good cheer and good things, as is attested by the following menu:

## The Moana Hotel.

### HONOLULU, TERRITORY OF HAWAII.

THE ONLY HOTEL IN THE TERRITORY OF HAWAII WITH PASSENGER AND FREIGHT ELEVATORS.

ALL ROOMS FITTED WITH TELEPHONE.

SLEEPING APARTMENTS ELEGANTLY FURNISHED, WITH PRIVATE BATH ROOMS ATTACHED.

THE DINING ROOM, WITH SEATING CAPACITY FOR OVER 300 GUESTS, PARTIALLY BUILT OVER THE SURF, OFFERS THE FULLEST BENEFITS OF OCEAN BREEZES.

THE HOTEL HAS ITS OWN POWER PLANT, OPERATING

OTIS ELECTRIC ELEVATORS,
OVER 1,200 ELECTRIC LIGHTS,
ICE MAKING MACHINERY,
COLD STORAGE CHAMBERS,
"TROY" LAUNDRY MACHINERY,
PATTERN 1900.

FORTY-EIGHT COMMODIOUS AND WELL EQUIPPED BATH HOUSES FOR THE USE OF GUESTS INDULGING IN SEA BATHING, SURF BOATING OR SURF-BOAT RIDING.

AMERICAN PLAN.    RATES $3.90 PER DAY AND UPWARDS.

### Moana Hotel Co., Ltd.
#### PROPRIETORS.

OF INTEREST TO TOURISTS.

There is a charm about the wonderfully equable climate that fascinates. On Waikiki Beach, Honolulu's principal suburb, the maximum temperature in 1901 was 89 and the minimum 56, the average being 72. These figures will not vary more than 4 degrees in twenty years. The sea water registers from 74 to 78 the year round. Some of the sights of the city are the Bishop Museum, Kamehameha Schools for Hawaiian boys and girls; Oahu College, with its old stone wall covered with wild night-blooming cereus, and the Capitol. Diamond Head and Kapiolani Park are within a mile of the Moana Hotel. Nuuanu Pali, Mount Tantalus and Punchbowl, all of them glorious view points, are reached by carriage drives and broad and perfectly maintained roads. Surf bathing on Waikiki Beach is enjoyed every month in the year. The city and its environs are liberally supplied with electric lights and telephones, over 2,600 of the latter being in use. An excursion into the country by rail-car or wagonette affords opportunities large sugar plantations and fields anas and pineapples.

Luggage tags, early 1900s.

# Baby Moana

Max Kuhn was an engineer at the hotel in 1902. Sadie was a Swedish nanny staying with a family at the hotel taking care of their daughter, Julia. Max and Sadie met, fell in love, and married. On Feb. 1, 1903, a girl was born to the couple in the Peacock Cottage next to the hotel. The baby was named Julia Moana (which means "broad expanse of ocean" in Hawaiian) Kuhn. Sadie soon became ill and the couple moved to California where Sadie later died. Baby Moana grew up in the San Francisco area. At age 16, she won a beauty contest. The prize was a trip to Hawaii or the equivalent in cash. She took the money and went to Hollywood. There she roomed and danced in chorus lines with struggling young girls like herself, who later went on to fame—Janet Gaynor and Joan Crawford. She was hired as a dancer and eventually acted in a number of silent movies. She retired from acting around 1929 or '30, at the end of her first marriage. She remarried and was with her second husband, Ralph Giffard for 46 years, but had no children of her own. It was 1972 before she again returned to her native Hawaii. She died of heart failure in 1981.

Baby Moana in a horseless carriage, circa 1904. MH

Julia Moana Kuhn as a movie star in
1925. MH

# MYSTERY AT THE MOANA

## *Was Jane Stanford poisoned the night of Feb. 28, 1905?*

BY GARY OGLE

W as it murder at the Moana Hotel?
Not according to high-born opinion in California. Only in Honolulu did doctors, scientists and police conclude that the prominent tourist had been a victim of a terrible crime. Nevertheless, it was the California version that eventually prevailed over that given in the small, far-away country.

It was Feb. 28, 1905, and the rambling, four-year-old Moana in Waikiki was still wearing its first coat of paint. One of the guests in residence was Mrs. Jane Stanford, widow of California Sen. Leland Stanford, founder of the university that still bears the name. That night, in Room 120 of the Moana, she died screaming in agony. And the cause of her violent death was diagnosed as strychnine poisoning.

The incident caused a sensation in Honolulu as well as in her home city of San Francisco.

Mrs. Stanford had arrived Feb. 15 in the islands and moved into the Moana. With her was a paid companion, Bertha Berner, and a maid, Mae Hunt, the two employees sharing Room 122.

Mrs. Stanford had come to Hawaii not merely to enjoy herself. She also sought to escape the possible repetition of a sinister incident that had occurred the previous month in San Francisco.

There, on the evening of Jan. 14, Mrs. Stanford drank her accustomed glass of Poland mineral water, noticing that it tasted bitter. A maid, Elizabeth Richmond, took a sip, agreed and gave her employer an emetic to induce vomiting. Mrs. Stanford soon felt better.

The next day, Richmond took the water to a drug store, but the pharmacist was unable to analyze it. He sent it to an assay office, which eventually reported that three-quarters of a grain of strychnine was left in the Poland water bottle.

Shocked that anyone would try to kill her, Mrs. Stanford discharged Miss Richmond immediately and hired the Morse detective agency to investigate. Fearing for her safety, she left the family mansion on Nob Hill to sail to Hawaii, while the household staff remained behind under surveillance.

A t 10 a.m. on Feb. 28, Mrs. Stanford, her maid and her companion embarked on a sightseeing trip and picnic which took them over the Pali. They stopped for lunch in a grove of trees, and nothing was amiss outside of the fact that Mrs. Stanford felt some stiffness after eating. She was helped to her feet by the surrey driver and Miss Berner.

Returning to Honolulu, they stopped to look at the Royal Mausoleum and then at Sach's Dry Goods at 116 S. Hotel St. There, Mrs. Stanford checked on a dress she was having made. They were back at the Moana by 4 p.m., and Mrs. Stanford went to her room to rest before dinner.

Miss Berner accompanied her employer to dinner about 6:30. They did not stay long in the dining room because Mrs. Stanford complained that the large picnic lunch had upset her stomach and she limited herself to a bowl of soup. After dinner, the two women walked out on the beach before returning to the hotel lanai to spend the rest of the evening talking to other guests.

Miss Berner later recalled that Mrs. Stanford was "in good and bright spirits that evening and had been all day."

At 8:30 p.m., Mrs. Stanford returned to her room. Like many others of her day, she habitually used numerous patent medicines before retiring. That night, she instructed Miss Berner to set out a teaspoonful of bicarbonate of soda from a newly opened bottle that had been packed in San Francisco, and a capsule of Cascara laxative. Miss Berner left her charge and went to bed at 9 p.m.

T wo hours later, Bertha Berner was awakened by cries from the next room. She ran into the hallway, where she found Mrs. Stanford leaning against her bedroom door, holding her stomach.

"Bertha! Mae!" she cried to the two women. "I am so sick!"

Miss Berner sent the elevator operator for a doctor and then helped the older woman into a chair. The woman was clearly dying.

Continual spasms and convulsions shook her body and her jaws became so stiff that Miss Berner had to massage them before Mrs. Stanford could open her mouth wide enough to sip warm water. She did manage to drink six or seven glasses to induce vomiting.

Within minutes, Dr. J. H. Humphris, resident physician at the Moana, arrived.

"Doctor, I think I am poisoned!" said Mrs. Stanford. Dr. Humphris immediately sent for a stomach pump.

Dr. Humphris relieved the spasms temporarily with a hypodermic injection, but within seconds a new, more intense attack came and Mrs. Stanford's body heaved in a final, giant convulsion.

"Oh, God, forgive me my sins!" she cried. "This is a horrible death to die!"

She fell back, dead, at 11:40 p.m.

Another physician, Dr. Harvey Murray, had arrived as the final attack began, too late to be of any help. Shortly after, Dr. F. R. Day clattered up with the stomach pump.

There was nothing anyone could do and Humphris ordered a carriage and drove into Honolulu to notify the sheriff.

The next day, the three doctors performed an autopsy, finding nothing to indicate a natural cause of death. Two government chemists also searched for poison in the body. Unofficially, they also told the sheriff there was strychnine in the bottle of bicarbonate.

Meanwhile, the mourning began. Hawaiian

women wove a lei as an expression of sympathy. Stanford University President David Starr Jordan announced plans to come to Honolulu to handle funeral arrangements. Mrs. Stanford's will was made public, and she had left most of her estate, more than $1 million, to her brother. And $15,000 to her companion, Bertha Berner.

The inquest began March 6 in the dining room of the Moana Hotel. The first witness was Miss Berner, whom The Pacific Commercial Advertiser (ancestor of The Honolulu Advertiser) described as a "remarkable woman" of "determined nature," and "marvelously well controlled."

Reporters also noted that Miss Berner, who had inherited a small fortune in the dollars of that day, "measured every word" and was "too engagingly frank."

Miss Berner described the earlier poisoning incident in San Francisco. She also explained that the fatal bottle of bicarbonate of soda had stood in an open room in the Stanford mansion for six days before being packed, and she traced the events of Mrs. Stanford's final day.

Other witnesses, including Mae Hunt and Dr. Humphris, told much the same story of the final hours.

A parade of doctors and chemists also testified, including some of the most respected medical and scientific names in the community. All seemed to agree that every symptom indicated a classic case of strychnine poisoning and even noted that a tiny amount of strychnine was found in the bicarbonate bottle.

A small element of doubt appeared, however, when one chemist reported he had also conducted tests on cascaret capsules similar to those the woman took besides the soda the night she died.

A tiny amount of strychnine, he announced, was a usual ingredient in these capsules—not enough to cause death or illness, but sufficient to cause the chemical discoloration that was observed in Mrs. Stanford's body during the autopsy, the discoloration which was given as evidence of poisoning.

Nevertheless, the medical testimony for poisoning was overwhelming and the coroner's jury decided in less than two minutes that Mrs. Stanford had died "from strychnine poisoning introduced into a bottle of bicarbonate of soda with felonious intent . . . "

Representatives of Stanford University, however, would entertain no suggestion of foul play in the death of the wife of the university's founder. President Jordan and the chairman of the board of trustees arrived in Honolulu and observed the inquest. As they left for San Francisco with Mrs. Stanford's body, however, they issued a statement saying that she had not been poisoned but had died of heart failure.

They said it was caused by angina pectorus brought on by overexertion during the afternoon picnic.

To explain the strychnine in the soda, the two university officials suggested it could have been mixed in by the pharmacist. Finally, in direct contradiction of the medical testimony, the educators insisted that the symptoms displayed by Mrs. Stanford during her last moments alive were inconsistent with strychnine poisoning.

The doctors who had performed the autopsy bristled. Humphris, Murray, Day and others repeated their conclusion that strychnine caused her death and detailed their reasons. They pointed out several scientific fallacies in the version given by the university officials.

It was Jordan's theory of Jane Stanford's death that prevailed, however, and the Honolulu Police Department dropped its investigation within weeks. No one was ever arrested for the murder.

A group of San Francisco doctors concluded on the basis of newspaper accounts there that "no evidence" proved Mrs. Stanford had been poisoned, and their opinion was accepted over the views of the Island doctors who were directly involved.

In time, biographical articles in encyclopedias and reference works all repeated the story that Mrs. Stanford had died of heart failure. And in 1935, Bertha Berner published a biography of Mrs. Stanford in which she argued the "natural causes" theory of her former employer's death. She made no mention of the decision of the coroner's jury and quoted only the newspaper-based investigation of the San Francisco doctors to support her conclusion.

But for the San Francisco poisoning incident, the death of Jane Stanford could be dismissed as a tragic mistake. But for the fact that she died a few weeks later, the San Francisco incident could be dismissed as mistake or a household prank. Together, however, the two incidents compel the conclusion by this author that not only was Mrs. Stanford's death due to strychnine poisoning, but that it resulted from foul play.

David Starr Jordan and others associated with him refused to acknowledge the persuasive evidence probably because as president of Stanford University, Jordan simply wanted to avoid any scandal.

The question of who killed Mrs. Stanford remains open, but the list of suspects must include everyone who had access to the mansion and to Mrs. Stanford's hotel room. Maids Elizabeth Richmond, Mae Hunt and Bertha Berner cannot be entirely above suspicion.

The case is made even more difficult because within a few months, the 1905 San Francisco earthquake and fire destroyed records in the pharmacy where the medicines were bought, those in the Morse detective agency, hired to investigate the San Francisco poisoning, and any information the San Francisco police had collected.

No one was ever charged with bringing about the mysterious death of Jane Stanford.

-15-

# MOONLIGHT AND RAINBOWS

*"The moonlight has been lovely beyond all telling these nights. As I have remarked, this is the rainy season, but Waikiki seems to be exempt from showers, and we have almost cloudless nights and days and sunsets and such rainbows. Anytime almost, that you look for one you can find a gorgeous rainbow."*

*Anne Goodwin Winslow*
*Fort DeRussy Days*
*January 8, 1909*

The Diamond Head wing being constructed in 1917. The Frank Hustace house is just to the right along with other beachfront homes. It is now the site of the hotel's Diamond Wing (the original Surfrider Hotel).

The porte cochere was decorated with flags for the opening of the two concrete annexes in 1918. MH

# THE BANYAN TREE AND COURT

The hotel's major symbol since its opening has been the famous Banyan Tree, a focal point of the Banyan Court. When Waikiki was mainly swampland with beautiful beaches, many people built stylish homes and bathhouses along the shore. To provide shade from the sun, people would plant kiawe (ironwood) shade trees which grew well in the sandy soil.

In 1904, Jared Smith, director of the Dept. of Agriculture Experiment Station planted a Banyan tree on the hotel's grounds. The tree is a ficus, a member of the fig family and originally came from Bengal, India, where it was considered sacred by the Indian Hindus. Its name is derived from Hindu traders called Banyans. It is a fast-growing tree that is easily propagated from cuts of itself and grows tall with a wide-spreading canopy.

When the hotel was built on the Peacock property, the Banyan tree became the focal point of the cool, beachfront courtyard where it provided shade by day and a romantic setting by night with its filtered starlight or moonlight.

In 1918, the two wings were added to the hotel and the tree was the center of the new Banyan Court from which the famous radio show, Hawaii Calls was broadcast from 1935 to 1975. The court was paved at the time and together with the lanais on its three sides, became a favorite dining and dancing spot for generations of visitors.

With the addition of a swimming pool and The Snack Bar in the 1989 renovation, the Banyan Court is again the center of hotel activity.

In 1979, the Banyan tree was among the first of Hawaii's rare trees to be placed on the Exceptional Tree List, a Honolulu City and County register created to protect rare or historic trees. The tree received a trimming and branch shaping in 1989 to produce windows in its limbs to allow sunlight to enter and enhance its growth. It is now an impressive 75 feet high with limbs extending 150 feet across and its trunk has a massive 40-foot circumference. Because the historic tree is protected under state law, a permit is required for the annual trimming necessary to keep the tree healthy. It takes seven skilled arborists several days to check the tree's root system and perform the ceremonial "haircut."

An early view
of the
Banyan
Court. MH

The Banyan
Court has been
the scene of
much social
activity for more
than nine
decades,
including the
popular radio
program,
"Hawaii Calls."
HA

The Banyan
Court in the
1950s. MH

A front view with the Moana cottages, circa 1930s. MH

This aerial view was taken by the U.S. Navy, Fleet Air Arm in the 1930s. The hills behind Waikiki were just beginning to be built up. MH

The beachside view with the Moana pier. The top view is in the early 1900s showing the house to the right that had to be removed to make way for the 1918 concrete wings in the bottom photo, circa late 1920s. MH

A beachside view of the hotel in 1915. The bathhouse that was in place before the hotel was built has been incorporated into the beachfront complex. BM R.J. Baker #34611

This later view, prior to 1918, shows the beachfront complex expanded and remodeled. MH

Top: Moana hotel stationery.
Below: This 1935 beachside view shows the remodeled
dining room and the removal of the old beachhouse. MH

## An Evening of Enchantment
### Mary Lydia Barrette
### Paradise of the Pacific 1926

*"Should you chance, in Honolulu on an evening, to find time hanging heavily on your hands, there is a place to go where even the most exciting will find interest and pleasure. Go to the Banyan Court of the Moana Hotel. Should it be a starlit night, it will be fascinating, for the stars seem to appear and disappear between the leaves of the giant Banyan tree, while the notes of the steel guitar and ukulele wave in and out...."*

Circa 1930s.

*Modest Cost enhances the perfect Vacation*

Guests have the choice of either American or European Plan. In either case the tariff is very reasonable.

### THE MOANA-SEASIDE HOTEL
#### ALL-YEAR RATES

EUROPEAN PLAN . . . . *Single, $4, $5 and $6 per day.*
(*without meals*) . . . . *Double, $6, $8 and $10 per day.*
AMERICAN PLAN . . . . *Single, $6, $7 and $8 per day.*
(*with meals*) . . . . *Double, $11, $13 and $15 per day.*
*Lower rates for permanent and semi-permanent guests.*
*All rooms have private or connecting baths.*

### THE ROYAL HAWAIIAN HOTEL

This famous hotel, situated nearby, adds its attractiveness to Waikiki, at the same time supplementing the hospitality of the Moana-Seaside by cordially inviting the latter's guests to all its public functions. Under the same management and ownership, it is operated on the American Plan only, with reasonable rates.

*Reservations, complete information and literature may be had by communicating with—*

#### MATSON LINE

New York, 535 Fifth Ave. : Chicago, 230 No. Michigan Ave.
San Francisco, 215 Market St. : Los Angeles, 730 So. Broadway
Seattle, 814 Second Ave. : Portland, 327 Southwest Pine St.

*or any steamship, railway, or travel agency.*

#### HAWAIIAN HOTELS, LTD.
Arthur Benaglia, *Managing Director*
*Honolulu, Hawaii*

*Operating:* The Moana-Seaside Hotel and Bungalows
The Royal Hawaiian Hotel · The Waialae Golf Club

PRINTED IN U.S.A.

A large crowd on the beach, possibly the start of a canoe race, 1916 or 1917. BM #93782

A good view of the beachfront and the Moana pier about 1925. MH

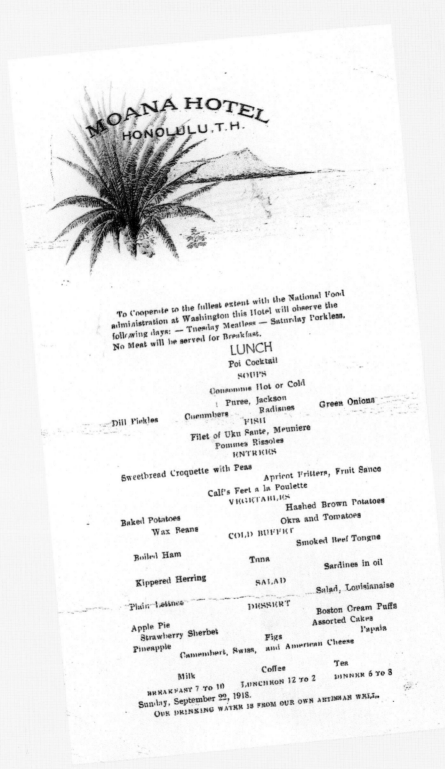

To Cooperate to the fullest extent with the National Food
administration at Washington this Hotel will observe the
following days: — Tuesday Meatless — Saturday Porkless.
No Meat will be served for Breakfast.

## LUNCH

Poi Cocktail

### SOUPS

Consomme Hot or Cold

Puree, Jackson

Dill Pickles     Cucumbers     Radishes     Green Onions

### FISH

Filet of Uku Sante, Meuniere
Pommes Rissoles

### ENTREES

Sweetbread Croquette with Peas

Apricot Fritters, Fruit Sauce

Calf's Feet a la Poulette

### VEGETABLES

Hashed Brown Potatoes

Baked Potatoes     Okra and Tomatoes
Wax Beans

### COLD BUFFET

Smoked Beef Tongue

Boiled Ham          Tuna
                              Sardines in oil

Kippered Herring

### SALAD

Salad, Louisianaise

Plain Lettuce

### DESSERT

Boston Cream Puffs
Assorted Cakes

Apple Pie                              Papaia
Strawberry Sherbet      Figs
Pineapple
          Camembert, Swiss, and American Cheese

Milk          Coffee          Tea

BREAKFAST 7 To 10     LUNCHEON 12 To 2     DINNER 6 To 8
Sunday, September 22, 1918.
OUR DRINKING WATER IS FROM OUR OWN ARTESIAN WELL.

This menu was issued on September 22, 1918, several months before the end of the war.
Notice the meatless days.

Hotel swimsuits from the
1920s and '30s.

The Prince of Wales on Waikiki
Beach. Notice the Moana swimsuit
that he has on. MH

An NBC broadcast of Honolulu station KGU from the beach in front of the Moana, no date. MH

An idyllic view of the beach prior to 1918. Diamond Head is in the distance. MH

A good view of the Moana Pier, built in the 1890s and torn down in 1930.
BM CD 25234 L.E. Edgeworth

CABLE ADDRESS "MOANA"

"An Evening Of Hawaii's Music"
Given under the auspices of Hawaii's Serenaders.
March 18, 1924.   Banquet Hall   8.30 P. M.

## PROGRAMME

| | | | |
|---|---|---|---|
| 1. | Hawaiian Serenade | "Aina Malihini" | Hawaii's Serenaders |
| 2. | Vocal Solo | "Makani Kaili Aloha" | Amy Awai Heleluhe |
| 3. | Special | "Hula Ku-i" | Baby Kaiponohea |
| 4. | Steel-guitar Solo | "Hawaiian Melodies" | Kid Walter Lane |
| 5. | Yodeling | "Puna Paia Aala" | Arthur Komomua & Hamau-Kaleo Trio |
| 6. | Double Quartette | "Imi Au Ia Oe" | Lawealilo Girls |
| 7. | Bass Solo | "Wiliwili Wai" | Sam Kaalonahi & Hawaii's Serenaders |
| 8. | Descriptive Dance | "E Liliu E" | Lorna Hauoli Awai |
| 9. | Tenor Solo | "Wahine U-i" | Bill Ewaliko |

10. Hula Dancing as follows: (1. Puili   3. Kakalaau   A. Kaoo's Dancers
 (2. Uliuli   4. Olapa

11. Solo & Chorus   "Old Plantation"   Amy Heleluhe & Hawaii's Serenaders

12. Hawaiian Act   'Na Lei O Hawaii"   Makaonaona Beauties
(An Act of eight Islands:   each island being represented)
(by a certain flower, Lei Wreath or as follows:

1. Hawaii Lehua      4. Oahu Ilima         7. Kahoolawe Hinahina
2. Maui Rose         5. Kawai Mokihana     8, Lanai Kaunaoa
3. Molokai Kukui     6. Niihau Pupu

13. Hula Song   "Tropical Hula Girl"   Keokionalani
14. Finale   "Aloha Oe"   Entire Chorus.

# Moana-Seaside Hotel and Bungalows

·

## A HOME CIRCLE OF CONTENT
## IN A TROPIC-ISLAND GARDEN

·

Put an ocean between you and the world of hurry and worry ... come to the Moana-Seaside Hotel! Gladden your days with a smiling Hawaiian sun, and tinge your evenings in a Coconut Grove with the romance that silvers from a tropic moon. Find the delicious seclusion of a South-Pacific island, yet keep close at hand all the things essential to gracious twentieth-century living. In other words, enjoy the kind of vacation only Hawaii can offer.

Nature has outdone herself in fashioning this Eden of beauty, raising gorgeous mountains from a turquoise sea, blanketing them with giant trees and ferns, garlanding them with myriad flowers. Graceful palms crowd almost to the water's edge. Here the fortunate visitor may take his ease in Hawaii's year-'round spring weather. Yet this secluded oasis of hospitality is only three minutes from Honolulu's stores and docks.

What Nature began the Moana-Seaside Hotel has completed. Into this ideal setting it has brought modern luxury. Magnificent public rooms furnish an artistic background for delightful social gatherings. Delicious meals are enjoyed in the spacious dining room close to the rim of world famous Waikiki Beach.

Hospitality is expressed *thoughtfully* in the ample proportions of the bedrooms and in the completeness of their furnishings, nearly all having private or connecting baths, and many of them have private *lanais*.

Just a few steps from the main entrance and situated in the midst of beautiful flower gardens, bungalows offer the seclusion of a private home, plus the advantage of being efficiently serviced by a skillful hotel staff.

Famous orchestras furnish excellent dance music on the Banyan Lanai. Then there are the entertainments of The Royal Hawaiian Hotel nearby, to which guests of the Moana-Seaside are also invited.

Hawaii's perfect all-year climate keeps outdoor life continually in the ascendent. Whatever sport you like best is always in season ... tennis, badminton, bowling, clock golf, archery, horseback riding, sailing, deep-sea fishing, motoring, and those sports found only in Hawaii—surf-boarding and outrigger canoeing.

Then there is golf ... over a sporty, championship course that is famous the world over. Guests of the Moana-Seaside enjoy all the privileges of the Waialae Golf Club. To play this course is like making a tour of famous clubs all over the world ... St. Andrews, Prestwick, North Berwick, National, Piping Rock, Valido, for every hole is a reproduction from some renowned course.

A beachfront view in the 1960s. By this time high-rises were beginning to appear in the Waikiki area. MH

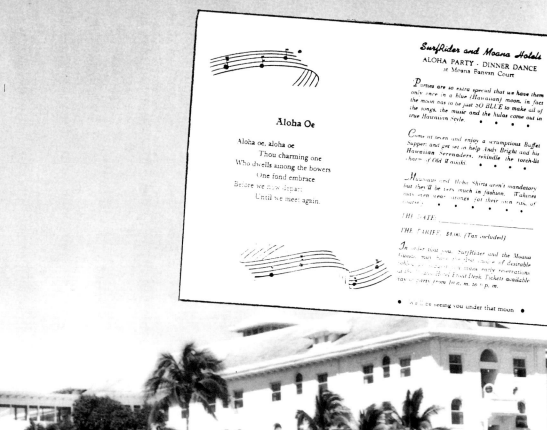

# JOHNNY NOBLE

One of Hawaii's best-known musicians and songwriters was long associated with the Moana Hotel. Johnny Noble, of English and Hawaiian descent, was born in Honolulu in 1892.

In his youth he became an outstanding whistler and also learned to play the piano and read music. His early schooling took him to San Francisco and St. Louis in Honolulu where he also mastered the guitar and drums.

After graduating from St. Louis (a private high school) in 1911, he started a career at the Mutual Telephone Company as a collector, a job he held for many years.

A local movie theater hired him as a drummer for their silent movies where he worked after his regular job. He also met A.R. "Sunny" Cunha, a local musician who wrote some of Hawaii's earliest songs. This led to a long association between the two musicians.

In 1918, Dan Pokipala had a band called the Moana Hotel Orchestra. Noble joined the band as a drummer, then as a piano player and finally became the band leader. Modern Hawaiian music was their specialty.

The first big hit for Cunha and Noble was "Hula Blues," written in 1920. That same year he played before the Prince of Wales (future King Edward of England) and his cousin Lord Mountbatten, who were staying at the Moana.

In 1921, Noble married Emilie Dunn and they had a daughter, Demetra, the next year. That same year he organized a Hawaiian orchestra for the Matson Line passenger ships, later to become the parent company of the Moana Hotel. He also wrote the music for his second big hit, "Ala Moana" and then formed a partnership with Bob Lukens and together they wrote many Hawaiian hit songs.

KGU became the first radio station in Hawaii in 1922 and Johnny and his orchestra began playing on it in May. The orchestra also played at the Waialae Golf Club, owned by the Matson Line, every Friday night starting in 1927.

In 1928, he signed with the Brunswick Company to provide musicians for their label. He then made a trip to San Francisco to broadcast Hawaiian songs with KPOA. While on the mainland he made a tour of the west coast with his band, the first of many mainland tours, which also included the Royal Hawaiian Girl's Glee Club.

By the 1930s, Noble had changed his music to the new Tin Pan Alley style, but he was getting tired of the travelling and holding down a full time job. He semi-retired in 1932 and became Director of Entertainment at the Moana and the new Royal Hawaiian hotels.

After Harry Owens took over Noble's band in 1934, Johnny's duties were restricted to booking bands and entertainment for the two hotels.

Besides writing dozens of Hawaiian songs during his career, Noble was the first member of ASCAP (American Society of Composers, Authors and Publishers) in Hawaii in 1935.

With increased defense preparations taking place in Hawaii in the late 1930s, Noble wrote a song named "The Blackout March," and after the attack on Pearl Harbor, he wrote "Remember Pearl Harbor," but another mainland composer wrote a tune with the same name which was published first.

During the war, Noble worked with the USO in his native Hawaii until his death on January 13, 1944. He left Hawaii with a music legacy that is still with us today.

Johnny Noble, 1932, at 40 years old.

DB

Johnny Noble and his orchestra, 1918. MH

Johnny Noble and his orchestra on the Moana Pier.

The Moana orchestra under the Banyan tree.

The music of "Hula Blues," Johnny Noble's first hit song.

"From the Banyan Court of the Moana Hotel overlooking
bee-you-tiful Waikiki Beach, it's...HAWAII CALLS!"

These words were first broadcast to 20 West Coast radio stations
on July 3, 1935. For forty years, Hawaii's most famous radio show
brought Hawaiian music to listeners around the world.

By the end of 1935, the show, emceed by Webley Edwards, had
gone national and at every broadcast an assistant would run out to the
shoreline with a microphone to send the "sounds of the waves of
Waikiki" to its listeners.

Harry Owens wrote the song title "Hawaii Calls" and Al Kealoha
Perry and his "Singing Surfriders" were heard weekly. Andy Bright
became famous for his rendition of "Hawaiian Cowboy" as did Alfred
Apaka. There was the comedy of "Squeeze Kamana," the appearance
of Hilo Hattie and Hawaiian dancers who were a regular feature.

The show originated in the hotel's Banyan Court but occasionally
would broadcast from other Waikiki locations.

Hawaii Calls records first appeared in 1952, and for a time in the
1960s, the program had a brief stint on television. At its peak of popularity in the 1950s, the show was carried by 750 radio stations world-
wide.

The Banyan Court and the Moana Hotel will always be remem-
bered as the "home" of Hawaii Calls.

DB

"Hawaii Calls" in 1959. HA

N⁰ 129

"Hawaii Calls"
Buffet
Luncheon

Date 11/14

Table No. 7L

Close-up view of the "Hawaii Calls" stage on the veranda of the Moana Hotel. MH

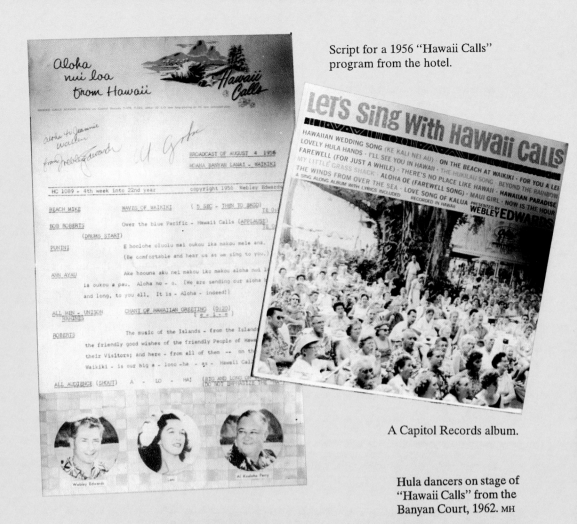

Script for a 1956 "Hawaii Calls" program from the hotel.

A Capitol Records album.

Hula dancers on stage of "Hawaii Calls" from the Banyan Court, 1962. MH

The "Hawaii Calls" troupe on the beach in front of the Moana. Webley Edwards sits on the outrigger, November 1954. Burl Burlingame Archive

DB

Hilo Hattie performs before an "Hawaii Calls" audience at the Banyan Court, circa 1950s. HA

Host Webley Edwards and entertainer Arthur Godfrey at the microphone of a "Hawaii Calls" broadcast from the Moana, circa 1950s. Burl Burlingame Archive

Broadcast program for
"Hawaii Calls" on July 9,
1966.

BROADCAST 06 JULY 9 1966
HAWAIIAN VILLAGE - WAIKIKI

---

*1607th broadcast (31 years 2 weeks) since Hawaii Calls started July 1935*
*HAWAII CALLS Reg. U. S. Patent Office  Copyright 1935, 1966, Webley Edwards*

[TE = Time Elapsed - estimate]

| | |
|---|---|
| EDWARDS<br>[WAVES] | The rustle of Waikiki's waves - [WAVES]  - the chant of Island girls - and this is a call - from Hawaii - |
| DRUMS<br>AND STRINGS | BEGIN SOUND OF DRUMS, STRINGS |
| PUNINI [up] | E hoolohe !  Oluolu mai oukou ika makou mele ana !<br>(Harken !  Hear us - and be comfortable - as we<br>sing to you !) |
| NINA<br>KEALIIWAHAMANA | Ake hoouna aku nei makou ika makou aloha nui loa<br>ia oukou a pau.  Aloha no - o !  (We are sending our Aloha -<br>big and long - to you all.  It is - Aloha - indeed yes !) |
| GIRLS | CHANT: E - I - E |

TE 0:35

| | |
|---|---|
| EDWARDS<br>[WAVES] | A great many people are with us here at Waikiki Beach - in the tropical long house of the Hawaiian Village. Bright Hawaiian colors in the flowers and flower leis - in the muu-muus and holokus - the visitors are wearing.<br><br>Hawaiian singers - just a lot of them ! - ready with songs of romance - and dreamy melody - and some in the high spirited rhythm that begins our music - as - Hawaii Calls! |

[START INTRO on "begins our music"]

| | |
|---|---|
| STRINGS [BKGD] | INTRO TO:  "KONI AU" |
| ALL AUDIENCE | A LO HA  [MORE SHOUTS]  [APPLAUSE] |

[1:05]

| | |
|---|---|
| CHORUS | KONI AU IKA WAI<br>[hula]  S ME MY DARLING |

[1:15]

# WAR YEARS

The defense buildup on Oahu began in earnest in 1940 after the Pacific Fleet was moved to Pearl Harbor from San Pedro, California. Thousands of defense workers poured into Honolulu to work at the navy yard and to build up the air and army defenses of the island.

The Moana, like other hotels at Waikiki and in downtown Honolulu filled up. There was tension in the air but no one foresaw the disastrous event that occurred on the morning of December 7, 1941. Many islanders remember "Hawaii Calls" announcer, Webley Edwards radio broadcast over KGMB at the time of the attack: "This is not a drill; this is the real McCoy!" he told his audience.

With this attack on Oahu by Japanese forces, all of Hawaii was on a war footing and martial law was declared. Barbed wire stretched across the beaches and blackout restrictions were enforced.

Matson's biggest hotel, The Royal Hawaiian on Kalakaua Avenue, was leased to the U.S. Navy as a rest and relaxation center, mainly for submarine personnel. The Moana however, remained open as a guest hotel, but was full all the time with servicemen or defense-related personnel.

One strange incident that took place at the hotel was described in Beth Bailey and David Farber's book, *The First Strange Place, Race and Sex in World War II Hawaii*. After the Pearl Harbor attack the ladies of the night from Hotel Street in downtown Honolulu moved all over town. One well-known madam, Jean O'Hara took two adjoining rooms at the hotel with two other ladies. One night the ladies had a party and invited some men in for drinking and dancing. The house detective came to quiet things down. The two ladies and the men ran to the adjoining room. O'Hara plopped on the bed, opened a book, and asked the detective to come in. He called the vice squad and only O'Hara was arrested. With martial law in effect she was taken before a military provost court judge who sentenced her to six months in jail for creating a disturbance at the hotel. This was a harsh sentence for the offense and she ended up serving only four months.

The hotel weathered the war years without too many changes. It was always full although it was hard to keep liquor stocked and to obtain certain food items because of shortages and rationing.

Some normalcy returned after martial law was lifted and a joyous day was had when the announcement was made that the war was over and Japan had surrendered.

## Schedule of Holiday Events, 1941-1942

☆ ☆

### AT THE ROYAL HAWAIIAN HOTEL

| | |
|---|---|
| WEDNESDAY<br>December 24 | Christmas Eve Dinner-Dance on Waikiki Terrace. Entertainment. Dinner-Dance $3.00. Dancing $1.00. |
| THURSDAY<br>December 25 | Christmas Dinner and Concert by Royal Hawaiian Salon Group. $2.50 per person. |
| SATURDAY<br>December 27 | Regular Dinner-Dance with Nite Club Entertainment on Waikiki Terrace. Dinner-Dance $3.00. Dancing $1.50. |
| TUESDAY<br>December 30 | Regular Tuesday Evening Dance CANCELLED. |
| WEDNESDAY<br>December 31 | Gala New Year's Eve Supper-Dance. Spectacular Floor Show. Favors and Gifts to the Ladies. $7.50 per person. |
| THURSDAY<br>January 1 | New Year's Dinner-Dance on Waikiki Terrace. Nite Club Entertainment. Dinner-Dance $3.00. Dancing $1.00. |

☆ ☆

### AT THE MOANA HOTEL

| | |
|---|---|
| THURSDAY<br>December 25 | Christmas Dinner and Concert by Royal Hawaiian Girls. Dinner $2.00 per person. |
| FRIDAY<br>December 26 | Regular Friday Evening Dinner and Dance. Dinner and Dance $2.50. Dancing $1.00. |
| WEDNESDAY<br>December 31 | New Year's Eve Dinner and Dance. Starting 8:00 p. m. Dinner and Dance $5.00 per person. Dancing only $3.00 per person. |
| THURSDAY<br>January 1 | New Year's Dinner and Concert by Royal Hawaiian Girls. Dinner $2.00 per person. |

# GALA NEW YEAR'S EVE PARTIES
### WEDNESDAY, DECEMBER 31, 1941

| ROYAL HAWAIIAN<br>Waikiki Terrace | MOANA HOTEL<br>Banyan Lanai |
|---|---|
| ☆ | ☆ |
| acular Cavalcade of the Dance<br>1912 to 1942<br>Including<br>TURKEY TROT, BUNNY HUG, CASTLE WALK, CHARLESTON AND OTHERS | DINNER - DANCE<br>FRANK ELLIS<br>And His Orchestra |
| KAALOA NOTLEY<br>Assisted by the Hula Maids, in Ancient and Modern Hulas<br>Presented by Boleyn-Anderson Studio | ☆ |
| | Dinner Served from 8:00 p. m. |
| Dancing from 8:30 p. m.<br>Supper Served at 11:00 p. m.<br>Giggie Royse and His Orchestra | Dancing from 8:00 p. m. |
| | Noise Makers    Novelties |
| Beautiful Souvenir Gifts Presented to the Ladies<br>Noise Makers    Novelties | ☆ |
| PRICE, INCLUDING SUPPER, $7.50 PER PERSON<br>Phone Assistant Manager - 9911 | PRICE INCLUDING DINNER, $5.00 PER PERSON<br>DANCING ONLY, $3.00 PER PERSON<br>Phone Assistant Manager - 9921 |

WE SUGGEST MAKING YOUR RESERVATIONS EARLY
(OVER)

# World War II Story

On a beautiful moonlit night in June 1943, I was at the Moana–not as a guest–but because our C-47 had just flown the previous night from Hamilton Field in California to Hickam Field in Honolulu. This was just at the turning point in the Pacific War, 19 months after Pearl Harbor (my 20th birthday, December 7, 1941).

One of our five crew members under Lt. Billy McLeod (I was his co-pilot) said that we must get out to Waikiki Beach and see the Moana Hotel. McLeod was a clever procurer and somehow he got a jeep and driver to take us from Hickam Field to Waikiki. It was after dark when we got there, but we were determined to swim off Waikiki Beach, just the five of us.

Looking back from chest-deep water at the stately Moana commanding that expanse of beach, seeing only the Banyan tree and other tropical foliage extending from ewa into infinity and over to Diamond Head, silhouetted in the moonlight (no lights as a blackout was in effect)...eerie but beautiful...yes, romantic.

Joe Salisbury
Twin Falls, Idaho

Waikiki Beach during wartime. View taken from the front of the Moana beachhouse with the Royal Hawaiian in the background. HA

The beach was a maze of barbed wire during the war but that didn't stop the enjoyment of the sand, sun and water. The Moana's dining room is the building on the left with Diamond Head in the background.

Photo by Werner Stoy

The Captain and Ship's Company
of the
United States Ship Arizona
invite

*Miss Mary La Croix*

to a dance to be given at the
Moana Hotel
Monday evening, September 22, 1941

Dancing from 8 to 12 o'clock

Please present this card

*E.C. Brasky — J.S.M.C.*

Invitation for a dance at the Moana on September 22, 1941, sponsored by the *U.S.S. Arizona* berthed at Pearl Harbor. Just two months later the *U.S.S. Arizona* would be destroyed and many lives would be lost.

MOANA HOTEL, HONOLULU, HAWAII.          FRIDAY, MARCH 31st, 1944

IMPORTANT: By order of The Foreign Funds Control Office, only the Hawaiian Series of United States Currency can be accepted in this Dining Room. Exchange must be made personally with the Hotel Front Office Cashier.

## DINNER
**$1.50 PER PERSON**

CHOICE OF ONE

Seafood Cocktail          Pickled Beets

CHOICE OF ONE

Moana Fish Chawder                    Consomme Tosca

CHOICE OF ONE

Filet of Halibut Saute, Meuniere

Breaded Veal Cutlet, Tomato Sauce          Boiled Calfs Tongue, Vinaigrette

American Pot Roast with Corn Fritters

Assorted Cold Meat with Potato Salad

WITH

Fried Egg-plant          String Beans in Butter          Boiled Rice

Rissolee or Boiled Hawaiian Rose Potatoes

Salads du Jour

CHOICE OF ONE

Blackberry Pie          Cabinet Pudding          Royal Anne Cherries

Coupe Moana          Sherbet          Swiss Cheese

Fruit Jell-o          Papaia          Sliced Pineapple

Coffee          Tea          Milk

* * *

MEAL HOURS: Breakfast 7 to 9.30;  Luncheon 12 to 1.30;  Dinner 5:30 to 8.
All prices listed hereon are at or below our OPA ceiling prices.
Patrons not in uniforms please wear coat at dinner.

WEDNESDAY, AUGUST 30th, 1944

# LUNCHEON
### $1.00 PER PERSON

### CHOICE OF ONE

Chilled Orange Juice     Poi Cocktail     Green Onions and Radishes

Lentil Soup Paysanne     Hot or Jellied Consomme

### CHOICE OF ONE

Poached Filet of Codfish, Portugaise

Curried Eggs on Rice Bengal

Little Pork Sausages, Country Style

Hungarian Beef Goulash with Spatzellis

All Vegetable Plate with Baked Papaia

Assorted Cold Meat with Potato Salad

Spinach en Branche     Zucchini Saute     Boiled Rice

Saute, Mashed or Boiled Potatoes

### CHOICE OF ONE

Peach Pie     Cabinet Custard     Preserved Prunes

Fruit Jell-o     Strawberry Ice Cream

Sliced Pineapple     Papaia

Pineapple Frappe     Coffee     Tea     Milk

**ALL PRICES LISTED HEREON ARE AT OR BELOW OUR OPA CEILING PRICES.**

Navy men seated around the Banyan Court in 1942. The Navy took over the Royal Hawaiian but the Moana remained in civilian hands. BM CD 102, 103 H. Bauer

The threat of another Japanese invasion was considered a possibility in 1942, even after the decisive Battle of Midway. By August the Federal government had withdrawn all regular currency used in Hawaii and replaced it with specially printed notes. These had "Hawaii" overprinted in large letters on the back and vertically at each end of the front. The old money was burned in a sugar mill at Aiea, and after August 15, 1942, it became illegal to possess, without a license, the regular notes. The reasoning was that in the event of an invasion, the new notes would automatically become invalid as they were restricted to Hawaii and the South Pacific area. They were free to circulate after October 1944, and were withdrawn by April 1946 when they were replaced with regular, old notes.

# THE BUILDING

By 1920, when this aerial photo was taken, the hotel was still the center of Waikiki. Most of the area was still swamp land and taro fields. The Ala Wai Canal had not yet been built. MH

A good aerial view of the hotel prior to 1950 showing the cottages opposite the hotel entrance, the extended restaurant on the beach and the bathhouse adjacent to it. HA

The Royal Hawaiian Hotel is under construction in this view from 1926. MH

The two prominent hotels of Waikiki in this aerial photo taken by the military on October 18, 1929, two years after the Royal Hawaiian opened. MH

The porte cochere and Moana cottages on Kalakaua Avenue, early 1930s. MH

The courtyard of the Moana cottages, 1930s. This is the site which the Sheraton Princess Kaiulani Hotel now stands. MH

The Moana cottages, directly across the street from the hotel, no date. MH

The Moana cottages were moved in 1953 and the land cleared for the new high-rise Princess Kaiulani Hotel. MH

Both photos shown here are now the location of the Grand Salon Ballroom.

The main lobby in 1914. MH

This 1914 view of the lounge is now the site of the hotel's main lobby. MH

An early view of the dining area that extended out onto the beach. MH

An early view of the veranda that opened out on the Banyan Court. MH

The dining room some time between 1911 and 1920. MH

These three views
of the lobby area
show the modern-
istic remodeling
done to the
hotel's interior in
the 1930s. HA

The front desk in early 1930s. MH

This view shows how the intricate columns were modernized. MH

More views of the lounge interior looking towards Kalakaua Avenue. MH

The former cocktail bar just off the Banyan Court before the reconstruction. This bar was located in what is now referred to as The Grand Salon (formerly referred to as The Kamaaina Bar, and later The Press Club). HA

Guest room interior, circa 1915. MH

Another view of the hotel in 1940, one year before Hawaii and the entire United States would be thrust into war.

BM CB 30824 R.J. Baker Coll.

Trolleys were still
operating on
Kalakaua Avenue
in the 1930s. MH

Moana exterior facing Kalakaua Avenue in the 1940s.
The ornate porte cochere has by this time been covered
over. Compare this view with the exterior photo on
page 16-17. BM30825 R.J. Baker Coll.

## Moana Hotel

### WAIKIKI BEACH
### Banyan Court

**SUNDAY, FEBRUARY 21, 1954**

★

WASHINGTON'S BIRTHDAY PROMISES YOU A GAY EVENING
. . . . FEATURING THE POPULAR AND DELIGHTFUL MUSIC
OF ANDY BRIGHT, WHILE DINING UNDER THE BANYAN TREE.

★

Dinner from seven to eight thirty.    Dancing from eight to midnight.

★

Reservations made in order received by calling the SurfRider or Moana
front desk.

★

$4.60 PER PERSON. ALL TAXES INCLUDED.

---

### Waikiki's
### Most Enchanting Evening

☆

## The Candlelight Dinner Dance
### UNDER THE BANYAN TREE
**MOANA HOTEL**

EVERY THURSDAY    DINNER FROM 7:30 P. M.
DANCING FROM 8:00 P. M.

WITH EXCITING ENTERTAINMENT
AND CHEF OSCAR'S
SPECIAL 4-COURSE DINNER

DINNER $4.65 (tax included)
RESERVATIONS REQUIRED.

---

**SATURDAY, December 22**

Hawaii Calls    Moana Banyan Court    Buffet  -    12:30 P.M.
Broadcast  -    2:00 P.M.
Santa arrival via canoe  -    2:30 P.M.
HULA SHOW (for camera fans). Reservations at front desk.

Polynesian Floor Show with Kent Ghirard   -   -   -    11:00 P.M.

**SUNDAY, December 23**

Concert By The Sea    Moana Banyan Court  -    4:00 P.M.

**MONDAY, December 24**

Choral Concert By Candlelight    SurfRider Lobby  -    9:00 P.M.
45 voices conducted by Mr. John Kelly.

Gluwein Punch Party    -   -   -   -   -   -    10:30 P.M.
For Moana-SurfRider Guests.

### Merry Christmas

**TUESDAY, December 25**

Manager's Eggnog Party  Moana Poinciana Room  -   12:00 - 1:00 P.M.
For Moana-SurfRider Guests.

Christmas Candlelight Dinner  Moana Dining Room  -   6:00 - 9:00 P.M.

**WEDNESDAY, December 26**

Lurline Guest Arrival   -   -   -   -   -   -    10:15 A.M.
Hula Show & Fashion Show    SurfRider Lawn  -    11:00 A.M.
Polynesian Floor Show    Moana Banyan Court  -    11:00 P.M.

### Lurline Holiday Cruise

**THURSDAY, December 27**

Aloha Party & Buffet Dinner    Moana Banyan Court    7:00 P.M.
Hawaiian, Tahitian, Samoan Entertainment, with
M. C., Sterling Mossman.    Dancing 'til midnight.

**FRIDAY, December 28**

No Host Cocktail Party    Moana Banyan Court    4:30 - 5:30 P.M.
Complimentary Hors D'Oeuvres.  Departure music for
departing Lurline Guests. Make reservations with Asst. Manager.

**SATURDAY, December 29**

Polynesian Floor Show    Banyan Court, Moana    11:00 P.M.

**SUNDAY, December 30**

Concert By The Sea    Banyan Court, Moana    4:00 P.M.

### Happy New Year

**MONDAY, December 31**

Cocktail Time —    Open to Public    5:00 - 7:00 P.M.
Wandering Serenaders    -   -   -    5:00 - 7:00 P.M.
Buffet Dinner    Moana Hotel    8:30 - 10:00 P.M.
Dancing    Moana & SurfRider Hotels  -    9:30 - 1:30 A.M.

Floor Show with M. C., Sterling Mossman    SurfRider  10:45 - 11:50 P.M.
Moana  11:15 - 11:45 P.M.
(Reservations at Front Desk)

**TUESDAY, January 1**

Manager's Eggnog Party    Poinciana Room    12:00 - 1:00 P.M.
For Moana-SurfRider Guests.

New Year's Candlelight Dinner  Moana Dining Room    6:00 - 9:00 P.M.

Dancing 'till Midnight    Banyan Court

To you
the

## Seasons Greetings & Best Wishes

*H. C. Donnelly*

# The Diamond and Tower Wings

Tourism was fast developing after the end of World War II with larger surplus military and new larger commercial airplanes being developed that could make the long trip over water to Hawaii. The Matson Steamship Company had put its tourist boats back in service from the mainland to Honolulu.

By 1950 Matson, the parent company of the Moana Hotel, decided to build a brand new hotel adjacent to their existing structure. Both the Moana and the Royal Hawaiian hotels were usually at capacity.

An eight-story hotel was decided on and groundbreaking took place in November 1950 on property originally deeded to the missionary physician, Jerrit Parmele in 1839 by King Kamehameha IV. It opened in 1952 and was named SurfRider Hotel for the surfriders who challenged the waves at Waikiki Beach.

In 1964, Japanese hotelman Kenji Osano paid $65 a square foot for another piece of the property to build this 21-story, 436-room addition. In 1969 the new Surfrider Hotel on the Honolulu side of the Moana Hotel was opened.

Ground breaking of the SurfRider Hotel on November 4, 1950. This building is now referred to as the Diamond Wing.
MH

All rooms have private lanais with 180 degree views of the beach and ocean. The hotel has a second-story porte cochere drive-in entrance from Kalakaua Avenue with a shopping arcade on the ground floor. The entire wing has 430 rooms, penthouses, a restaurant, cafe, lounge, and banquet facilities.

After this structure was completed it was named The Surfrider and the older SurfRider was renamed the Ocean Lanai Wing. This wing is now called the Diamond Wing, the Surfrider is named the Tower Wing, the original Moana Hotel building and its two 1918 wings are the Banyan Wing. The entire complex, all connected into one, is now called the Sheraton Moana Surfrider.

The construction of the new SurfRider Hotel commenced in 1950. MH

The eight-story SurfRider under construction in 1951. BM CP 115, 614

# 1989 Restoration

The desire to return the hotel to its 1918 appearance began as a simple plan in 1983 to update the lobby and public areas, and eventually evolved into a master plan to restore the entire hotel. A $50 million, 20-month historic restoration resulted in a gala re-opening in March 1989.

Under the careful direction of Joint Venture Architects, with Virginia D. Murison, AIA of Honolulu as principal architect and interior designer, the restoration involved the exact duplication of the 1901 architecture and replication of those features to be returned to their authentic state.

The original 1915 drawings of the Moana's wing additions were discovered at the Royal Hawaiian. These, along with period photographs, provided details on the reconstruction of the original porte cochere.

Under many coats of paint were found ghosts of porthole windows and plaster fleur-de-lis decorations. Templates for the original decorative plasterwork and sample castings of the column capitals were found in the basement. The replacements were hand-carved in the Philippines.

The Roof Garden, which had been converted to guest rooms, was reconstructed and a grand staircase and rotunda were replaced in the Banyan Wing. The hotel was repainted in its original off-white and grey colors.

The Banyan Court was redone, the tree trimmed and a swimming pool and snack bar added. The Surfrider was also remodeled and it and the Ocean Lanai Wing were connected to the original building to create a beachfront resort.

The guest rooms in the original hotel combine the best of the old world traditions with modern conveniences. All rooms feature the woods originally used on each floor, including oak, mahogany and maple. For the top two floors, cherry and the rare Hawaiian wood, Koa, are used. For the first time in history, air-conditioning was installed in each room. A Colonial reproduction armoire with a television and refrigeration unit graces each Banyan Wing room.

Complementing the Moana's restoration is a second floor Historical Room, displaying a variety of memorabilia from the hotel and Waikiki area.

In recognition of its extensive historic restoration project, the Sheraton Moana Surfrider has received a number of local and national awards including—a National Preservation Honor Award, Hawaii Renaissance Award and a Restaurant/Hotel Design International 7th Annual Design Award.

million historical
restoration in
1988. MH
David Franzen Photo

The Moana Hotel and its two auxiliaries, the Ocean Lanai Wing on the left and the Surfrider on the right, in the 1970s. The front awning extended to the sidewalk at this time. MH

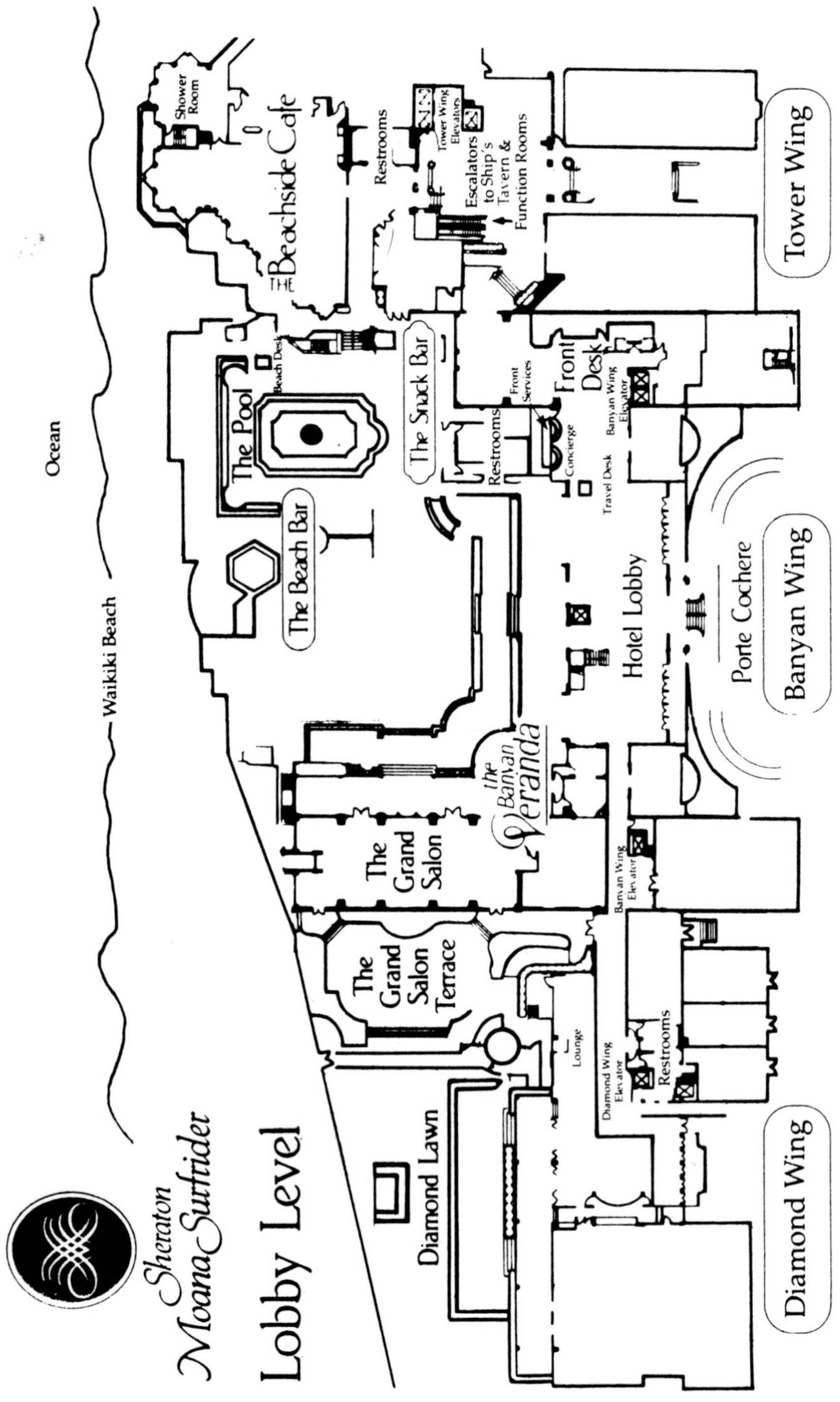

Sheraton
Moana Surfrider
Lobby Level
Ocean
Waikiki Beach
Kalakaua Avenue
Shower Room
THE Beachside Cafe
Restrooms
Tower Wing Elevators
Escalators to Ship's Tavern & Function Rooms
Tower Wing
Beach Desk
The Pool
The Snack Bar
Front Services
Front Desk
Banyan Wing Elevator
Restrooms
Concierge
Travel Desk
The Beach Bar
Hotel Lobby
Porte Cochere
Banyan Wing
the Banyan Veranda
The Grand Salon
The Grand Salon Terrace
Banyan Wing Elevator
Lounge
Diamond Wing Elevator
Restrooms
Diamond Lawn
Diamond Wing

The Ship's Tavern dining room (top) and entrance (bottom). MH Franzen Photography

# COLOR VIEWS

A nighttime view of the
porte cochere facing
Kalakaua Avenue.

The beautiful restored
lobby area.

Sheraton Moana Surfrider front desk.

The hotel's Historical Room has a vast array of artifacts, photos and a short video on the history of the Moana and its Waikiki environs.

The Banyan Court, Banyan tree and Banyan Veranda.

David Franzen Photos

The front colonnade facing Kalakaua Avenue.

The Banyan Veranda.

A close-up view of the restored Ionic columns.

The Parlor.

The Ballroom Foyer.

A typical restored room
in the Banyan Wing.

The famous Moana Banyan tree.

Exterior view.

A view of the Diamond Lawn area.

A modern view of the beach in front of the Diamond Wing. Diamond Head is in the background.

# BIBLIOGRAPHY

Acson, Veneeta, *Waikiki, Nine Walks Through Time*, Island Heritage Limited, Honolulu, 1983.

Allen, Gwenfread, *Hawaii's War Years*, University of Hawaii Press, Honolulu, 1945.

Bailey, Beth and David Farber, *The First Strange Place; Race and Sex in World War II Hawaii*, The John Hopkins University Press, Baltimore, MD, 1992.

Brown, DeSoto, *Hawaii Recalls, Selling Romance to America, Nostalgic Images of the Hawaiian Islands 1910-1950,* Editions Limited, Honolulu, 1982.

Brown, DeSoto, *Aloha Hawaii, 100 Years of Pictures from Hawaii's Most Famous Beach,* Editions Limited, Honolulu, 1985.

Cohen, Stan, *The Pink Palace, The Royal Hawaiian Hotel, A Sheraton Hotel in Hawaii,* Pictorial Histories Publishing Co., Inc., Missoula, MT, 1986.

Miller, Ray & Jo, *Hawaii "....Wish You Were Here,"* The Evergreen Press, Avalon, CA, 1994.

Sheraton Moana Surfrider, *Moana Memories, Postcard Book*, Mutual Publishing, Honolulu, 1989.

Wisniewski, Richard A., *Hawaii: The Territorial Years, 1900-1959, A Pictorial History,* Pacific Basin Enterprises, Honolulu, 1984.

Worden, William L., *Cargos, Matson's First Century in the Pacific,* University Press of Hawaii, Honolulu, 1981.

Plus an extensive article in the May 1990 issue of *Hospitality* Magazine and other magazine and newspaper articles.

## About the Author

The author is a native West Virginian and a resident of Missoula, Montana. He has been in the publishing business for 23 years and is the author/co-author of 65 books and has published over 200. He has written four other Hawaiian books, *East Wind Rain, A Pictorial History of the Pearl Harbor Attack; Hawaiian Airlines, A Pictorial History of the Pacific's Pioneer Air Carrier; The Pink Palace, The Royal Hawaiian Hotel, A Sheraton Hotel in Hawaii* and *Princess Victoria Kaiulani and the Princess Kaiulani Hotel in Waikiki*